D0638578

The Wonderful World
Of Grandmothers

The Wonderful World Of Grandmothers

Writings By and About Those Very Important Persons

Edited by Jan Miller Gilmore

Illustrated by Nadine Bernard

HALLMARK EDITIONS

LIFE'S NEW LOVELINESS

Life has started all over for me —
The young years of happiness
Have come again in a sweeter form
Than a mother could ever guess;
The love and devotion I gave my child
I thought I could give no other,
But life held a lovely surprise for me —
I became "Grandmother!"

KAY ANDREW

February 28, 1978

Happy Birthday, Grandma! I
hope you like this book. I
love you bunches!

With hugs and kisses,
Rebekah Marie
XXX OOO

THE WORLD
A GRANDMOTHER SHARES

The world shared by a grandmother
and grandchild is always filled
with wonderful moments, special memories.
Dr. Margaret Mead reflects upon the world
she shared with her grandmother and the one
she hopes to build with her granddaughter.

On October 9, 1969, I became a grandmother.

Curious! Through no immediate act of my own, my status was altered irreversibly and for all time. It is always so, of course. The birth of a child, an extraordinarily small and fragile creature, changes one's own place in the world. . . .

My granddaughter is named Sevanne Margaret Kassarjian. . . . They call her Vanni. . . .

Now, fully inducted into the status of "Grandma," the name I called my grandmother and my daughter called my mother, I think back to myself as a child with my own grandmother.

The grandmother who lived with us was my father's mother. Looking back, I see that she gave me an extra century . . . through the tales she told me about the little town of Winchester, Ohio, where she had grown up. Although it was 60 years before I myself saw Winchester, Grandma made every person, every house . . . familiar to me.

She read me books she had read as a child, and books my father had read. She told me . . . how times had changed. She explained to me about the telegraph, the first automobile and the men who were then just beginning to link far places in a new way, by flying.

All her life my grandmother had been a teacher, experimental, curious and exploratory, avid for new ideas on how to open the minds of small children. She taught me algebra before arithmetic, and wherever we went for our summer holidays she had me make a herbarium, using new methods to preserve the colors and outlines of plants.

She talked and I listened, and I talked and she listened. Later she used to tell me that after I had chattered to her all day, when evening came and the day's work was done, I would say to her in an expectant voice, "Now let's sit down and talk."

It is hard to know which is more important for a grandparent to do—talk or listen. But adults must keep time—the years before the child was born—firmly in mind. . . . She knew exactly what I knew and what had to be explained to me. She kept the rhythm of my life in her head. . . .

Since her [Vanni's] birth we have had an eclipse of the sun. Later I must not ask her if she remembers. She was still too young, younger than my brother was when he was wakened in the night to see Halley's comet— and the next day recalled nothing about it. But my grandmother knew that I did remember when she told me about other comets or when a meteor fell through the nighttime summer sky. She always remembered and differentiated among what had happened in my life and in my father's life and what she alone of all of us in the house had actually experienced.

I hope I shall remember in the same way just who Vanni is and what she can remember, so that I can make real for her my past and her mother's childhood, and in doing this give her the time depth she will need . . . .

She will never know a world without television carried by satellites and bringing messages from the moon, as her mother never knew a world without radio or without warfare shadowed by the bomb and by man's new responsibility for the whole planet. But Vanni will also discover a world that is only now emerging, and I shall understand it partly through her responses to it. . . .

Grandparents need grandchildren to keep the changing world alive for them. And grandchildren need grandparents to help them know who they are and to give them a sense of human experience in a world they cannot know. . . .

THE PERFECT GRANDMOTHER

*The following children's-eye views
of what a grandmother should be are
from "How to Succeed as Grandma"
by Dorothy Barclay.*

Obviously there are as many different ways of being a grandmother as there are women who qualify for the designation. Some overwork the part; some simply walk through it in a detached kind of way. But what do children think grandmothers ought to be? What do they like as visitors in her home? . . .

"A good grandmother is calm and quiet," an 8-year-old boy said. "You never see her do the shopping, but there's always good stuff to eat. She's not busy all the time. And even when she is busy, she's not *so* busy. You can come in the kitchen when she's cooking and she'll talk to you."

"You can have fun at a grandmother's house," a 6-year-old boy reported. "She isn't always telling you 'watch out.' She has ideas about things to do and she takes you places. Also she lets you spend your dollar for what you want. But if you spent it all for candy she wouldn't let you eat it all at once."

"I have three grandmothers," a worldly 7-year-old told us. "The one I like best has lots of things that are different, not like what we have at home. She gives me my milk from a pitcher that's like a rooster and all her dishes have different flowers painted on them. She has a lot of things I have to be careful when I touch. They are very pretty."

"My grandmother can talk about things that happened a long time ago," a 10-year-old observed. "When she was a child they didn't have television or jets. They had trolley cars instead of buses. She remembers the day World War II started. She has books my father read when he was little and a knife and fork he used when he was my age . . . .

. . .

The chief occupation of a grandmother's first year is to keep her hands off.

MRS. R. C. STURGIS

MY OWN SMALL FOOTNOTE

In this letter to her grandchildren, actress Helen Hayes discusses a very special gift only grandmothers can give their families.

My Dear Grandchildren:

At this writing, it is no longer fashionable to have Faith; but your grandmother has never been famous for her chic, so she isn't bothered by the intellectual hemlines. I have always been concerned with the whole, not the fragments; the positive, not the negative; the words, not the spaces between them. I loved and married my Charlie, your grandfather, because he was both poem and poet. What wonders he could work with words.

From your parents you learn love and laughter and how to put one foot before another. . . .

No one can tell me that man's presence on earth isn't expected — even announced. Because the magi come to each new babe and offer up such treasures as to dazzle the imagination. For what are jewels and spices and caskets of gold when compared with the minds and hearts of great men?

What can a grandmother offer in the midst

of such plenty? I wondered. With the feast of millenia set before you, the saga of all mankind on your bookshelf, what could I give you. . . ? And then I knew. Of course. My own small footnote. The homemade bread at the banquet. The private joke in the divine comedy. Your roots.

This, then, is the grandmother's special gift — a bridge to your past. It goes back, of course, to the beginning of time, but I cannot give it substance until my entrance. After all, I am the star. . . .

Heaven knows my life hasn't always been wise and faultless. It is a pastiche made up of opposites, of lethargy and bossiness, of pride and guilt, of discipline and frivolity. It hasn't always been a model and worthy of imitation, but it was round and it was real and I lived it all greedily.

Your grandmother is an actress who has spent her working life pretending to be gay or sad, hoping that the audience felt the same. More often than not I succeeded. Offstage, I was not always in such control. The technique of living is far more elusive. Alas! One does her best and, like Thornton Wilder's Mrs. Antrobus, I have survived.

Cast by the fates as Helen Hayes, I have

played the part for all it's worth. Child, maiden, sweetheart, wife, and now grandmother. We play many parts in this world and I want you to know them all — for together they make the whole. Trials and errors, hits and misses, I have enjoyed my life, children, and I pray you will, too. . . .

What are little grandchildren
              made of?
Some good and some bad
              from Mother and Dad.
And laughs and wails
              and Grandmother's tales.

I love you. *Grammy*

A WEEKEND VISIT
BY THE GRANDCHILDREN

I love my grandchildren, without a doubt—
I'm at my best when they're about!
But I'm not as young as I used to be,
And when they come to visit me,
After one little crisis on the heels of another—
I'm happy they can go home to "Mother"!

LOIS BAILEY

ON BECOMING A GRANDMOTHER

*The proud moment when "Mother"
becomes "Grandmother" holds an excitement
all its own. Here Dorothy Brandon recounts
the experience of Mamie Eisenhower's mother,
Mrs. Doud, as her first grandchild is born.*

Admittance to the hospital was by Army form —and more forms. Mrs. Eisenhower was in labor, but the nurse at the desk made her answer a string of questions so that a card could be filled out. It was all in slow motion, exasperating to Mrs. Doud whose experience in bearing children told her there was no time to waste. Finally the nurse murmured a room number and pointed down a high-ceilinged corridor. As Mrs. Doud started to go with Mamie, who was bravely picking up her suitcase, the nurse announced in bitten-off words that in *military* hospitals, the relatives of patients were permitted in rooms only during stated visiting hours.

Mrs. Doud gave the nurse a withering look and stalked down the hall after her daughter. They entered the ... room to find a great gritting and groaning coming from the general direction of a woman tossing in one of the beds.

Mrs. Doud stared in disbelief; surely Mamie, an officer's wife, would have privacy...!

She did not speak until her daughter was prone, then announced she was going to find a doctor—fast. At the door she almost collided with a young man in white, who started to give her a bit of his mind for her infraction of the rule: "No relatives are—" Fiddlesticks on Army regulations, cried . . . Mrs. Doud; what kind of regulations forced a patient to find her own room and put herself to bed—when the baby might be coming any minute? . . .

Still scrapping mad, but knowing her place was in the waiting room, now that the doctor had taken charge, Mrs. Doud retraced her steps down the corridor and sank with great weariness into a chair. The glare of the newly risen sun hurt her eyes, so she lowered her lids. . . .

The doctor's voice broke Mrs. Doud's reverie. He said with professional dispassion that Mrs. Eisenhower was coming along just fine. There was no reason to expect the baby before noon, so there was plenty of time for breakfast —and a walk. . . .

It was nearly half past eight when she was whisked back to the hospital . . . . Prepared to spend the rest of the morning in the lounge,

Mrs. Doud crossed the lobby toward a comfortable chair. Three steps, and she was confronted by a radiant nurse. Wasn't it wonderful to be the grandmother of a fine boy!

Grandmother! Boy! Mrs. Doud was fit to be tied. Her normally rosy complexion glowed like a well-stoked grate; she glowered at the nurse.

"I was insensible," she says. "I had been cheated out of the greatest moment of my life, I've never gotten over it . . . ."

WHAT A GRANDMOTHER IS

A grandmother is a lady who has no children of her own, so she likes other people's little girls. A grandfather is a man grandmother. He goes for walks with boys, and they talk about fishing and tractors and like that.

Grandmas don't have to do anything except be there. They are old, so they shouldn't play hard or run. It is enough if they drive us to the market where the pretend horse is and have lots of dimes ready. Or if they take us for walks, they slow down past things like pretty leaves or caterpillars. They should never say "Hurry up."

Usually they are fat, but not too fat to tie the kids' shoes. They wear glasses, and they can take their teeth and gums off. It is better if they don't typewrite or play cards, except with us. They don't have to be smart, only answer questions like why dogs chase cats or how come God isn't married.

They don't talk baby talk like visitors do, because it is hard to understand. When they read to us they don't skip words or mind if it is the same story again.

Everybody should try to have one, especially if you don't have television, because grandmas are the only grown-ups who have got time. PATSY GRAY, AGE 8

. . .

Was there ever a grandparent, bushed after a day of minding noisy youngsters, who hasn't felt the Lord knew what He was doing when He gave little children to young people?

JOE E. WELLS

SHE UNDERSTANDS

A grandma's 'bout the nicest thing
A feller ever had;
She seems to understand and care
Even when I'm bad.

She never seems a bit surprised
When I fill my pockets with mice;
She never makes me wash my ears,
She never calls me twice.

She always sits and reads to me,
The kind of stories I like,
And she doesn't think I'm a bit too young
Even for a two wheel bike.

She bakes me cookies, the nicest kind,
With raisins and nuts stuffed inside;
And she never says, "Now don't eat too much."
She just lets me decide.

A grandma's 'bout the nicest thing
A feller ever had;
But I wonder why she says so much,
"Buster, you're *just* like your dad!"

PHYLLIS C. MICHAEL

VINEGAR OR BEESWAX

Sometimes grandmothers rule
with an iron hand to conceal a heart of gold.
In Sterling North's novel So Dear to My Heart,
Granny Kincaid wrestles with her conscience
to reprimand her grandson or yield
to his pleas to keep a newborn black lamb.

At the corner of the springhouse she tore a
stout switch from the willow tree, and, pull-
ing it through her work-calloused hand,
stripped the tender new leaves and catkins
from its supple green length. . . .

But as she stepped into the big room of the
cabin where she had been both mother and
father to Jeremiah since cradle-rocking days
. . . her heart almost misgave her. There in
the pool of lamplight on the wide hearth Jeremiah had made a bed for his lamb in the
hickory-splint kindling basket, lining it as
best he could with warm flour pokes and dish-
cloths.

Steeling herself for the thrashing, she said,
"Jeremiah, it's my bounden duty to chastise
you. Take down your pants."

Jerry drew the lamb closer and looked up
with pleading eyes as Granny put the lantern

on the warming oven.

"I'm ready for my lickin', Granny," the boy said, "but please kin I warm and feed this little feller first?"

"Tryin' to git around me, ain't you?"

"Ain't never run away from a switchin' yet.". . .

"Wal," Granny said, hanging her shawl on its hook, "you got it comin' and yer agoin' to get it 'fore you go back to bed. Furthermore, I'm aputtin' my foot down and you ain't agoin' to keep that lamb."

"But first, Granny. . ."

"Oh, all right. . . ." She placed the switch within easy reach on the table.

From the battered copper teakettle singing on the range she poured a dishpan of hot water, cooled it from the water pail, and tested it with her bared elbow. . . .

"Black sheep give the most wool, Granny."

"Fiddlesticks. . . ."

"Aw, Granny. You kin make me a black homespun shirt."

"Never keered for old black wool offen an old black buck sheep."

"Look, Granny, he's feelin' real pert . . . !"

"Looks real puny and ailin' to me. Here, dip him in this warm water."

"Oh, thank you kindly, Granny . . . . Look, he likes it . . . . I'll feed him clover. He'll get so big and fat and strong."

"And mean and ornery," Granny added. . . . "Dry him with this flour poke, Jerry. His bottle's ready."

She tried the milk for temperature again. . . . Jerry saw with his own unbelieving eyes that Granny herself offered the eager lamb the nipple. . . .

"Where would you be keepin' him?"

"Here in the kitchen."

"How you gonna feed him?"

"Bottle-feed him on this here bottle. . . . Oh, Granny, please?"

"I reckon."

"You reckon you will?"

"I don't reckon I won't," said Granny; "leastways till he's big enough to roast."

"Oh, Granny. Yer the best granny," Jerry said, kissing the wrinkled cheek which just now had a salty tear upon it. "Give me my lickin' now, 'cause I won't hardly feel it I'm so happy."

"Bother," said Granny, breaking the willow switch and throwing it into the fireplace. "I'm gettin' softer'n beeswax." She wiped her eyes on a corner of her gingham apron.

A GRANDMOTHER'S PRAYER

Oh Lord, I do not ask for much,
Eternal beauty or youth or such:
Just give me a little hand to hold,
And I'll forget that I'm growing old.
I do not ask for cloudless skies,
A life that's free from tears and sighs:
Just give me a little face to kiss,
And anxious moments will turn to bliss.
For what is there, really, that means so much
As little hands that reach and touch,
As little eyes that search and see
Only the best in fragile me?
So let me grow more loving and wise
By looking at life through their wide eyes,
For through these little ones, You have given
This grateful grandmother a glimpse of Heaven.

BARBARA BURROW

IN DEFENSE OF GRANDMOTHERS

*Because a grandmother must sometimes
be a disciplinarian as well as a friend,
she occasionally must perform unwelcome
duties. Helen Southwick recounts
one moment she will always regret.*

For many years I have felt that someone should come to the defense of grandparents....

"Oh, he learned that from his grandparents," parents so often explain loftily, when Junior misbehaves. "They spoil him, you know."

Or: "I am so afraid his grandmother will slip something into his diet which he shouldn't have!"

Or: "Yes, we left the children with their grandparents this summer, but I dread the homecoming. They'll be completely demoralized. They always are. Their grandfather insists on treating them to ice-cream sodas and movies, and their grandmother always buys them unnecessary toys."

"Perhaps," sighed one young mother, in an obvious effort to be understanding, "it is rather difficult being a successful grandparent."

Perhaps, indeed....

When her grandchildren come to visit her, the grandmother must be not only a grandmother, but a hostess as well; and not only a hostess, but a dietitian and disciplinarian.

Her duties as a hostess are enormously complicated by the fact that her guests are not adults who may be relied upon to take care of themselves. They are children, and they are not her own children. If one of them does come to harm, the responsibility falls with double weight upon her.

And a grandmother's duties as disciplinarian and dietitian are complicated by the fact that she is understudying her own daughter, whose methods, for the moment, must be accepted as correct. . . .

Taking care of other people's children is hard work. However conscientiously the deputized caretaker may attempt to adhere to the training the children's parents have given them, it is always difficult to decide when to make an exception.

I recall, with regret which the years have not diminished, that I once stopped a game of "Button, Button, Who's Got the Button?" because I feared that a young mother would be upset if she returned and found that the children left in my care had stayed up past their bedtime. It is true there were extenuating circumstances. I had already made two attempts to separate them from their playfellows, and — unable to resist their plea that they had "just got started" — had twice postponed the distasteful task. At a half hour past their bedtime I again went outdoors, determined to be ruthless, if necessary. I found a row of little children sitting with cupped hands, waiting blissfully for the next move in the game. The moonlight shone upon their upraised, expectant little faces and I rudely shattered that lovely moment with the dictum that it was time for bed. It is not the scornful glances of the neighbor children, or even the heartbreaking sobs of the two I carried off to bed, which torture my memory still. It is that lovely, silvery moonlit moment of time which I destroyed, and can never replace, the little game which was destined never to be finished — the unnecessary disappointment to a half dozen little hearts — all that a regular bedtime hour might be kept. . . .

A GRANDMOTHER'S
SPECIAL LOVE

What could be more precious
Than a grandmother's special love—
She always seems to know the things
That we are fondest of,
She's always ready with a smile
Or a loving word of praise,
Her laughter always brightens up
The cloudiest of days,
She has an understanding heart
That encourages and cheers,
The love she gives so freely
Grows deeper with the years,
Her wisdom and devotion
Are blessings from above—
Nothing could be more precious
Than a grandmother's special love.

MARY DAWSON HUGHES

GRANDMA AND THE SPEAKEASY

*Grandmas can be an inspiration and
an education. Here Ted Peckham recalls
how his grandma "educated" him
during the Prohibition Era.*

As Grandma's "son" and escort I enjoyed beer foam, sarsaparilla, and root beer in some of the best speakeasies in Chicago, Cleveland, and New York. The "son" subterfuge was for the benefit of snoopers and busybodies who might want to know who we were, and this would throw them off the track. It was just as well on Mother's account, too. If word had reached her that her boy was frequenting a Madison Street speakeasy, even under Grandma's protecting eye, she would have thrown several kinds of fits, and certainly would have put a stop to these delicious excursions.

One afternoon . . . [we] went to a very nice, respectable speakeasy in an old boarded-up saloon on Madison Street, between Dearborn and Clark, where Tom Moore, one of Grandma's roomers, was bartender. He was very handsome and ruddy-cheeked, and he knew us well, for we came there often. We knocked, and a mysterious eye looked us over through a peephole, something that always gave me a chill down my spine, even though I knew the welcome we would get was always hearty.

We had hardly got inside and sat down, in fact the foam was still hissing on Grandma's beer mug and I hadn't yet had time to lick off the top (my special treat), when there was a terrific crash and we saw the bright blade of an ax come through the peephole panel in the door. Before we could move, the room was full of policemen. A raid! Grandma whispered excitedly, "My land, it's the Feds!" Tom Moore's harmless and delightful place was pinched.

A man in a tight-fitting, shiny suit, and wearing a derby that had seen better days, waved his arms and yelled, "Keep your seats, ladies and gentlemen, please keep your seats." He was talking to Grandma and me, because it was midafternoon and so far we were the only patrons. And his request came a little too late. Grandma and I had headed for the windows in the ladies' room and I had one leg on the way to freedom.

I was almost out the window when one of the raiders looked into the ladies' room. "Hey, Sarge!" he yelled, seizing me and hauling us both back into the outer room.

The sergeant stared at Grandma and at me.

31

"Madam," he said sternly, "what are you doing here?"

Grandma stared right back at him. She always did hate foolish questions. Couldn't he see the glass of untouched beer on the table?

"What's a lady doing breaking the law? And a little boy along, too!" he thundered.

His righteous air made no impression on Grandma. Dramatically she lowered her wonderful blue eyes, gave a great sigh, and remarked sadly, "I've been looking all over for my husband. I don't know where he is, and he hasn't been home in three days. Tom Moore is an old friend of ours. . . . I just stopped off to ask his advice about what I should do. . . ." her words broke off and she gave a convincing sob. I was fascinated, and almost believed her myself.

The sergeant was impressed, too. He patted Grandma's shoulder in sympathy and led her to the front door. "There now, ma'am, I hope you find your husband. I knew you weren't a lawbreaker."

Grandma put one last fillip on the scene. "Thank you, officer. You're *so* kind!" Then we scuttled off around the corner and peeked back to see Mr. Moore and his helper go off in the wagon. My main regret was that we missed the ride in the wagon, which was just like the one in the Keystone Cops. Grandma was disgusted, too. She hadn't even got to drink her beer.

IN FAVOR OF OLD-FASHIONED GRANDMOTHERS

Virginia Brasier applauds the many virtues of the old-fashioned grandmother.

The "old-fashionedness" of a grandmother— the kind I have in mind—is tranquility, maturity and a strength that the younger members of the family can rely on. Perhaps that sounds like matriarchy. But matriarchy also denotes rulership. The old-fashioned grandmother of story and of fact, too, gave advice when it was asked. She seldom laid down a law, or at least seldom made any firm requests. When she did, she was heeded. But kindness was her keynote.

Two things I would like to have when I am a grandmother are a smile and a very wide-skirted dress for the children to hide behind. I would like to have lots of good sense and tolerance, and the ability to peel an apple with a paring knife and keep the circular, spring-shaped paring unbroken. I hope I can make being old seem a marvelous thing, and if my fingers are curled a bit with rheumatism . . . or if I walk with a cane . . . I want my grandchildren to think it is interesting and extraordinary—and ask me how I manage to do it! . . .

Of course, I conceived my pattern for grandmothers from my own. We never knew Father's mother because she died when he was a young man. When he married, he adopted Mother's mother, too. So she did double duty. And she was everything a grandmother ought to be. She was a tall, broad-shouldered Scotswoman who came over to Canada a bride when she was 16.

Grandmother wore great, full, black dresses and a little gold watch on a chain and a black bonnet with sequins and feathers and a bigger black moire dress for Sunday church. But in all that black she never looked severe. She had candy in her workbox and lavender in her handkerchief box. . . . She made us count ten when we got angry at each other, and she fixed us endless slices of bread and butter sprinkled with granulated sugar—despite the fact that Mother thought it bad for our teeth.

And Grandmother hid us back of that voluminous skirt, one on either side, when Mother tried to catch us for a scolding. Everyone ended up laughing!

She was fortunate that she owned her own home and sensible enough to refuse any but a short visit to her daughters' who often begged her to come and stay. No wonder everyone wanted her! All her grandchildren, as well as the elders, adored her. Our young adoration, unfortunately, ran to begging for an endless succession of Grimm's fairy tales until her eyes were tired out. But I think the elders loved her because she never criticized any of them. As a matter of fact, she had a good word to say for everyone. . . .

But mine wasn't the only grandmother like this. There were — and are — many such grandmothers. . . .

To children the word has wonderful and delightful meaning: it means someone who loves you but never blames or punishes you. . . .

A grandmother can tell Johnny or Mary to wash his or her hands, or to spend more time reading, or to stand up straight, or not-to-eat-any-more-you'll-be-sick. . . .

A grandmother can spoil and pet and encourage and bind up wounds of the spirit and praise-to-the-skies and be an admiring audience and an infinite lot of other things that mothers are not expected to be. She can do it, not only to her grandchildren, but to her grown-up children too. Not to mention a whole host of friends, and even strangers. . . .

So a grandmother must be a harbor of quiet and freedom from blame; a refuge where children can get a straighter and longer view of life as they munch on things that aren't absolutely the best in the world for them. . . .

There is absolutely nothing to take the place of a good, old-fashioned grandmother. She may do a little harm now and then by spoiling her grandchildren, but nothing bad ever came from real love—even an overdose of real love. . . .

THE BEST TIME IS ALWAYS NOW

Sorting through mementoes
Of the children, long since grown,
It amazes me to think
They now have children of their own.

I don't feel that much older
'Way down deep inside;
Life's still a joy, a challenge
That I face with love and pride.

I wouldn't change a day I've lived,
Or live through it again;
It's enough to have the memories now
Of the children way back when.

And how lovely when their children now
Share with me some joy or other,
And how sweet to hear them call me
By my newest name "Grandmother."

MARY R. HURLEY

A BATH AT GRANDMA'S

*The Saturday night bath at Grandma's
has become an American legend.
In this selection Bertha Damon recalls
those "good old days."*

Under Grandma's administration a bath was
no fillip to begin the day on. It was a stern
duty, an almost impossible achievement, the
final hardship of a week of hardships.

First, the water must be drawn from the old
well, sixty feet from the kitchen door and
twenty feet deep . . . .

Next, all these pails of water must be emptied into great iron kettles and hung on the
iron crane to heat. The fire will need replen-
ishing. Out the back door, around the corner
of the house, down the flag walk to the side
gate, and across the road, is the woodpile. It is
where it is because there it is handy for men
folks to dump loads of wood direct from the
cart when they are hauling it once a year.
Saves them and the horse. Of course, it is most
unhandy for women folks to fetch from, several times a day, but unhandiness for women
folks never influenced the layout of country
barns or houses.

Grandma had her best callers trained to stop by the woodpile and bring in an armful of wood as they came. This scheme often relieved them from the necessity of rapping on the door; when they attempted that, the sticks fell down and made such a clatter even on the windiest nights, that it was heard inside, and the callers were let in just as promptly as if they had succeeded in rapping . . . .

Next, a room in which to bathe apart from the family must be warmed. More wood brought in for the fireplace there. Then must be assembled the big tin bathtub in the form of a pear-shaped coffin, towels, a mat, and homemade soap maintaining through strong sassafras overtones a dominant odor of household grease. Finally, the big iron kettles of hot water are lugged in and poured into the tub; the door is shut tight; the moment has come. Make of it what luxury you may before the water gets cold and your emergency fire goes out.

But your bath is not over; do not think it. All this soapy water must be emptied into pails, carried outdoors and emptied again. Then for a week all you have to do is to anticipate the next bath holiday or, if you prefer, six days' holiday from baths.

THE LANTERN

Supper dishes finished,
Gram went making calls
eager for some gossip;
bundled up in shawls,
mittens, fascinator,
against the evening chill;
carrying a lantern
to light her down the hill.

When it came eight-thirty,
we'd begin to pass
casually on errands
which took us by the glass,
watching for a distant
glimmer.

Now and then
a star looks like that lantern
coming home again.

FLORENCE JACOBS

GRANDMA AND THE BUCK DEER

*Grandmothers aren't always sweet
and gentle. Here Joel M. Vance writes
of his plucky grandmother's reaction
to finding a big buck deer in her tool shed.*

We were sitting at the breakfast table . . .
when we heard my grandmother shout. Most
women would have screamed but my grandmother wouldn't have screamed if Franken-
stein's creature had invaded her kitchen. . . .

But it was clear that something drastic was
wrong in the backyard and we all raced for
the door at the same time. . . .

"What's going on, Momma! What's the
matter. . .?"

"There's a great big buck deer in there!"
she exclaimed in a tone of utter disbelief. "I
think he's eating my washing!"

Her absolute outrage would have been funny except for two things: First, I had an
instant flash of prescience. I knew exactly how
that deer had gotten in there. It had followed
the faint tobacco trail to the shed and I had
shut him in the preceding night. . . .

Second, this was my grandmother, beside
whom Charles de Gaulle is a wishy-washy old

woman. If she ever found out I was behind or had anything to do with the current problem, she undoubtedly would insist that my mother put me up for adoption. . . .

"Hold him, Momma! Let me get my gun!" Uncle Al sprinted back across the yard. . . .

He was back in a flash. . . .

Feverishly he levered a shell into the chamber and raced across the yard. "Move aside, Momma! I'll let him out and we'll drop him!"

"Don't shoot him!" I yelled at the top of my voice, stung by an impulse which I regretted instantly. . . .

I could see my grandmother's face, something like that of Theodore Roosevelt on Mt. Rushmore, only not as pleasant. Storm clouds played around her granite brow. . . .

She knew I was behind the whole thing. She began a steady march across the yard toward where my mother and I stood. . . .

The buck charged through the open shed door . . . and headed for what looked like open country. Unfortunately, my grandmother had advanced to a point precisely between the buck and what the buck considered open country. The fear-crazed animal bore down on Grandma from the rear.

Both my mother and . . . Uncle Al shouted

a warning and my grandmother turned. As she whirled, the deer reached her. With fantastic reactions for a woman of that age, she grabbed the buck by his antlers and hung on grimly. She back-pedaled nimbly as the buck reared and plunged. . . . She held his head down so he couldn't use his hooves and danced in front of him as he moved her along by brute strength.

Uncle Al raised his gun, aimed and then lowered it helplessly. "Ah, Momma!" he cried in anguish . . . "Hold still! I can't hit the thing with you movin' like that!"

Even in her desperate plight, she threw him a look which would have shriveled asbestos. . . . At that instant, they passed the pickup truck and my grandmother, seeing a slender chance, let go and clambered with mountain goat agility up on the hood.

The buck, seeing he wasn't going to get Grandmother, returned to his original plan of putting a lot of distance behind him. . . .

She [Grandmother] slid down from the hood of the . . . truck and stood beside it trying to regain both her strength and her monolithic composure.

She looked up, took a deep breath that nearly cleared the yard of oxygen, and beckoned to me. It looked like the finger of the Grim Reaper.

"How did that deer get in my shed?" she asked in a measured, reverberating voice which could easily have been coming from the sky, accompanied by flashes of lightning and boiling black clouds. . . .

"I didn't put it there." Strictly speaking, that was true. I was evading and she knew it. . . .

"Child, you are going to get the worst whipping of your life!"

Suddenly my mother stepped between us. "Now just a minute, Mother," she said with steel in her voice. "I want to remind you that this is my son and if there is any disciplining to be done, his father and I will do it. You may be able to impose your will on me, but you're not going to do it to my children. Is that clear?"

She and her mother stood locked in a struggle of will which normally my grandmother would have won hands-down. But my mother, her child threatened, showed her heritage with an exhibition of inflexible will of her own. . . .

Later that night, my mother and my grandmother made up.

"Mother," I heard my mother say with, if

it's possible, a twinkle in her voice, "I think I'd like some venison for supper."

There was a long silence.

"Are you absolutely certain they didn't switch babies on you in that hospital?" my grandmother asked. But she didn't sound serious.

At least, I don't think she did.

YOUNGER EVERY DAY

I hear some people say grandchildren make them feel older. I guess I've never felt old at any time, least of all with grandchildren. Each one of them's got his own world. Four-year-old Clare has her world and Walt's got his, and 2-year-old Jane certainly has her world. When I get together with them and join a little bit in each of their worlds, I just can't help feeling a lot younger. . . .

MARIE FAZACKERLEY

THE BEST REMEDY
A GRANDMOTHER COULD HAVE

As a remedy for the blues, Bertha Beck
follows her doctor's orders and takes
a look at why her grandchildren love her.

My doctor has prescribed for low times. . . .
He says I am to sit down and list my more
admirable qualities—the things people defi-
nitely like about me. He says this does wonders for the morale. . . .

Right away I remember a small band of
followers who admire me unreservedly: my
grandchildren, all under six.

Why do these kids like me?

They like the way I behave as if I were
their age. The things that excite them excite
me, and I can laugh wholeheartedly at a lot
of the things they laugh at. . . . They make me
feel right young and carefree.

The way I don't care how much of a mess
they make in my house, provided they let me
help clean up before they go home. (My asking to help works better than asking *them* to
help me. . . .)

The way I casually put an arm around
them when they arrive for a visit. I make them

welcome and they're all set to enjoy me. But we don't get effusive. We say Hi.

The way I'll read them any story they ask for. They listen avidly for mistakes, hoping I'll change something or leave out a word so they can joyously correct me.

The way they have to teach me their songs over and over because I can't seem to get the words right. The way I tell them about their mommy and the things that happened when she was as young as they are. The way I hold my tongue in the corner of my mouth when I help build a skyscraper of blocks, because I am as scared as they are that the whole magnificent edifice will come tumbling down.

The way I sneeze 10 times when I eat ice cream . . . don't always know better than they do . . . think each grandchild has 10 birthdays a year, occasions for contriving treats and impromptu presents . . . .

I could make other lists, too, of course. I could itemize what my grandchildren don't like about me, and some things I don't enjoy about them. But that is not what the doctor ordered. . . .

Besides, for this moment, I have decided that there can't be any more fun in the world than having grandchildren.

CHANGING TIMES

Grandmothers are getting younger according to the following exchange between a child and his grandmother.

It happened late Thanksgiving afternoon as the family sat about the dinner table eating the last of the nuts and raisins. The youngest member, aged 4, spoke up.

"Gram," he asked, "are you really my grandmother?"

"Gram" assured him that she was, followed through with the inevitable "What made you ask that?"

"Because," said the youngest member, on whose sharp eyes a new holiday dress and freshly set permanent were not wasted, "grandmothers are supposed to have white hair and nose glasses and a rocking chair and paint Christmas cards. You don't look like a grandmother at all."

Pleasantly flustered at this gallantry, "Gram" reminded the young gentleman not to believe all the pictures he saw in advertisements, or in story books either. "Times change," she told him, "even with grandmothers . . . ."

NOURISHMENT FOR THE HEART

*A grandmother's love is unselfish
and enduring. Margot Benary-Isbert
discusses this special love.*

The day will come when we must let the
grandchildren go as we had to let the children
go. They'll proceed on their way, and we can
only hope that it will be the right way. If I
have been able to give them some nourish-
ment for heart and soul, I'll be satisfied. Never
is the love of the older generation returned by
the young ones with the same measure. Still, I
cannot quite agree with the remark of a
friend, that each love of an old person to a
young one necessarily turns out to be an unhappy love. In my vocabulary "love" and
"unhappy" are words that don't fit together.

BIOLOGY, I LOVE YOU

Oh, Friday night is here again,
And now, as oft before,
My grandsons and their sisters
Converge on Grandma's door.
It's time to bake the gingerbread
And wipe the noisy nose,
And let the tots play dress-up
In Grandma's funny clothes.

Come see the tent of Grandma's sheets,
The train of Grandma's chairs!
Come see the bread and jelly
On Grandma's shiny stairs!
Come join the sport; no frown of mine
Tonight shall spoil their fun;
Thank heaven they have two grandmas —
And I'm the other one.

IRENE CARLISLE

53

GRANDMA'S SABBATH PREPARATIONS

In this selection Gertrude Berg writes
of her grandmother's preparation
for the traditional Sabbath celebration.

I was close to her not only because I loved her
but also because she lived just around the
corner. Our two houses on Lexington Avenue
were separated in the rear by an areaway.
From my bedroom window I could look out
and down and see her living-room window.
That was more fun than the telephone. Every
morning when I was going to school, I used
to lean out of my window and call to her,
"*Yoohoo, Bubeshu, vif'l a zeyger iz es?*"
"Grandma, what time is it?" I could have
looked at the alarm clock, but it was more fun
to ask her. She always came to the window,
looked up at me, with her happy face, and told
me it was time to get dressed.

I would run over to her house on the way to
school, for no reason except to see her, say
hello and good-bye. She never said good-bye
back, only asked me if I was coming over later.
She knew I would, but she understood how
much I liked the ritual.

Friday visits, morning and afternoon, to

her house were the best. In the morning I would walk right into her kitchen full of confusion. The whole room was a mixture of dough drying for noodles, pots boiling, and the wooden kitchen table sprinkled all over with flour. It was like a rehearsal in a theater. The stage was being set, the props arranged, and the acts run through for this Friday night supper that was ten or eleven hours away and would be the finished performance. The only thing in the whole kitchen that wasn't in a mess was Bubeshu.

And when I came back from school and walked into Grandma's kitchen for the second time that day, it was like walking into another set. The place shone. It was as if nothing had gone on the whole day except polishing pots and waxing furniture. How such a frail little woman could do so much was something I tried hard to understand. On those rare days when I stayed home from school and watched her, I began to get the idea: it was continuous, calm, unhurried, well-organized, hard work. Staying home from school was a pleasure — especially on a Friday. If I could convince my mother that I was just a little sick and didn't have a temperature, I could run over to my grandmother's to watch and help.

Preparations for the Friday night dinner began so early in the morning that by the time I was up and dressed and had gotten to Bubeshu's the shopping was already done. The fish had been bought and cleaned, the chicken was plucked, and the dough for the noodles was rolled out and drying. There were no ready mixes in those days and few other time-saving conveniences or machinery. What you did, you did yourself, with some help from your whole family.

Grandma was busy filleting pounds of carp, pike, whitefish, and a species called "buffle." (I never did find out what kind of fish "buffle" was. There must be a definition someplace, but where?) These were the ingredients of gefilte fish that were chopped by hand in a wooden bowl that made a sound like music, then mixed, seasoned, and very slowly cooked by Bubeshu. She was also tending to the noodles for the soup and making the soup too. I loved to watch her little, plump hands fold the dough, pat it down, and then cut it up into noodles with those quick little slicings that only a really professional cook can manage.

While everything was quietly cooking, that's when the housecleaning began. There was nothing that didn't get picked up, dusted, cleaned, or polished. The sinks in the kitchen and even the bare pipes were all given new pleated calico skirts to hide them, as if they were going out in public. Even the quarter meter for the gas had a little skirt. By four on Friday afternoon the table was set, the house was spotless, and the food was ready, simmering or cooling.

Grandma never complained about her eighteen-hour working day. She acted as if it was her pleasure instead of her chore. The only time she seemed tired was when she would sit down, put her head up against her hand and lean on the kitchen table for a few moments. She always told me that this was the sweetest time of the day for her.

. . .

I consider the happiness of being a grandmother much overrated. How it can make any woman of experience happy to stand by and see her sons and daughters mismanage their children, I have never yet been able to understand. MRS. DE LA PASTURE

THOSE GOLDEN HARVEST YEARS

A lighthearted look at herself and her family
has made Rollie Hochstein decide that
the harvest years are, indeed, golden.

My mother is looking awfully chipper lately. Her eyes are bright; her complexion is rosy; her smile is dazzling and there's a spring in her step.

I, on the other hand, am looking wintry. After a day of refereeing the older children (in between bouts with a baby who won't stand still), I feel and look like last week's half-melted snowman.

"Are you Grandma's mommy?" my five-year-old asked me not so long ago.

"No," I told her. "I just feel that way."

That exchange set me thinking. Of all the double-barreled words in the English language, none is more to the point than that one. A grandmother is a mother who is having a grand time because her children are grown up. My eldest child being seven, I have an excellent chance of getting there in fifteen years. I can hardly wait.

By that time, my handbag will no longer be stuffed with PTA notices, broken shoe laces, spare mittens, popped buttons, pediatrician's prescriptions, teething biscuits and coupons to be mailed with fifty cents for a free cardboard racing car, unassembled. I will carry only snapshots of my grandchildren. . . .

My car will be free of car seats, car beds, diaper-changing kits, ballet costumes, ice skates, rock collections and children to be picked up and delivered on a day-long schedule. I will have plenty of room and plenty of time to take my grandchildren driving — when I'm in the mood. . . .

When my mother became a grandmother, she was a middle-aged lady. I remember the day she came breathlessly into my hospital room, tears of joy in her eyes. "My baby!" she cried. Only it wasn't me she was looking at.

She took up residence outside the nursery window and has been, ever since, my children's best friend and most outspoken admirer. By the time my third baby arrived, my mother was no longer middle-aged; she had grown young. . . .

When I was a child, candy and chewing gum were forbidden fruit and bedtime was never postponed. Now the disciplinarian of my youth pleads with me: "Let them stay up just fifteen minutes longer." She never arrives without an armful of gifts and goodies, never leaves without a headful of ideas for future gifts. She is never too busy to read a story or too tired to play first base. And she never says No.

Does Grandma spoil my children? You bet!

That's a grandmother's pleasure and privilege. And even though I may sound as if I don't believe it, it's great for the youngsters, too. I remember with warmth and joy the grandparents who spoiled me. I'm glad my children can bask in the sunny side of an easygoing, easygiving, carefree grandmother. And they reciprocate.

Grandma days are special. Nobody strays far from home when my parents are expected. When my parents' car pulls up, you can hear the shouting for blocks. Even the baby crows fit to burst her romper buttons.

Naturally, I can't expect my children to be so enthusiastic about me. I'm here all the time and I've got work to do. But as I said before, in fifteen years or so, I hope to be a grandmother myself.

"You're having a pretty good time," I remarked to my mother the other day.

"Yes I am. . . . This is my harvest."

I know just what she meant.

Set in Waverly, a linotype version of Walbaum.
The typeface was designed by Justus Erich Walbaum
(1768-1839), who was a typefounder at Goslar and at Weimar.
Printed on Hallmark Eggshell Book paper.
Designed by Lavonia Harrison.